# Twilight:
## Awaking the Stars

*Poems of the Night's Light*

I0091155

## GARY W. BURNS

*Turning Corner Books* ™

WWW.TURNINGCORNERBOOKS.COM

Published by:
**Turning Corner Books**
PO Box 121
Haymarket, VA 20168

Library of Congress Control Number: 2010927201
ISBN: 978-0-9845342-7-2

Sixth Printing, April 2023

Manufactured in the United States

Designed by the author; artwork by the author unless otherwise
noted.

- Jacket Photo and Section 1 Cover Photo: California Coast,
  USA; by Tammy L. Burns: Used by Permission
- Title Page Photo; The Pinwheel Galaxy, NASA image,
  Public Domain
- Page 25 Photo, Cancun, Mexico; by the Author

## Other Books of Poetry
## by Gary W. Burns

*Bridges: To There*
*(Poems for the Mind, Body & Spirit)*

*Clouds: On the Wind*
*(Poems for the Soul – A Meditation)*

*Earth Tones: A Journey*
*(Poetry for the Journey)*

*Garden Walks: Hand In Hand*
*(Poems To Relax By)*

*Moments: This to the Next*
*(Poetry – Now and Eternity)*

*Poems of Love: A Selection*

*Rainy Day: Wondering*
*(Poems for a Rainy Day)*

*To You With Love: Selected Poems*

*To Janny Lehman Litow*
*Poetry Editor*
*Ladies Home Journal*
*1979*

ೞ ———————— ೞ

*For her kind*
*And guiding words*

# CONTENTS

❖ *TWILIGHT*

Prelude 17

Blue, Twilight, Night 18

Anticipation 20

Wedded 21

In the Breeze 22

In Ease 23

By the Shore 24

Rejoice 26

Moonbeams and Things 27

Vision 28

Ever Be 29

## ❖ *LAMPLIGHT*

| | |
|---|---|
| At 1 AM | 33 |
| Ray of Hope | 34 |
| Lamplighter | 35 |
| Go Slow | 36 |
| Nighttime | 37 |
| Flickering Flame | 38 |
| Intention | 39 |
| Metamorphosis | 40 |
| Poetry | 41 |
| Turns | 42 |
| Into the Night | 43 |

## ❖ *INTO THE NIGHT*

Clear Night                       47

With the Light of the Night       48

Counting                          49

Dream-light                       50

Stargazing                        51

There Goes Midnight               52

Night Storm                       53

Wanting Eyes                      54

Faith                             55

Wholeness                         56

Each Night Through                57

Let Love Come                     58

Goodnight                         59

❖ *STARLIT*

All Starry Eyed                63

O the Love                     64

Stellar                        65

2:22 AM Yellowstone            66

The Wading Pool                68

Heavenly                       69

Moondrops                      70

Tranquility
   In *Twilight: Awaking the Stars*   71

As Lovers Say                  72

If You Listen Close            73

Midnight Eyes                  74

Passages                       75

Dream                          76

In Turn                        77

## ❖ *NIGHT TO TWILIGHT TO BLUE*

| | |
|---|---|
| Understanding | 81 |
| To . . . | 82 |
| Going Along | 83 |
| Of Memories | 84 |
| Matrix | 85 |
| Daylight Moon | 86 |
| Eclipse | 87 |
| Awareness | 88 |
| Of Troubling Clouds | 89 |
| Wind Chimes | 90 |
| Go On | 91 |
| Kindness | 92 |
| The Aegean | 93 |
| Dream By Dream | 94 |
| Life's Invite | 95 |
| Worth the Doing | 96 |
| Mi Amor | 97 |
| Epilogue (From the Mooring) | 98 |

# Twilight

## Prelude

Night came on,

Shy -

It blushed
Across the sky.

## Blue, Twilight, Night

*1*

Dawn,
Another day.

*2*

Morning,
Continuing
In ever repose
Slips away.

*3*

Midday clouds
Fill the sky
Echoing
In variations
Within my eye.

*4*

Light,
Fades away -
Night
Wraps
Everything
In sight.

*5*

Another day,
Gone.

## Anticipation

Rounder than the full of moon,
Softer than the kiss of night,

More gentle than the butterfly
In flight;

With daylight gone
And night's song
Near on,

In
Anticipation

Love
Waits.

## Wedded

Twilight's
Wedded to change
Eternally

And so we

## In the Breeze

Something in the breeze
Leads me to believe

The present
Is ever,

The willingness
Of wonder

## In Ease

In ease
Give way
To night and day;

For come what may
They take us
On our way.

## By the Shore

At twilight,
Holding hands,
We went along the shore,

As lovers often do.

As darkness grew
The evening sun
Lit
The lamp of the moon.

Soon,
The soft light
Was guiding our way
Through the inviting night.

## Rejoice

We,
Pouring
The warmth
Of love,
Toast one another
In celebration
Of us.

## Moonbeams
## And Things

Oceans of people
Sway
As tides
By nature do.

## Vision

Vision,

Looked at one way
Night's coming on
Looked at another
Somewhere
It's dawn

The bidding
Of our thought
Sees
What may please

## Ever Be

Come dance
With me.

My footwork's
Light,
Lively,
And free.

Yours eternally,
*Eternity*

# Lamplight

# At 1 AM

*1*

As the sun spun
Its' spinning way
To be the light
Of someone else's
Day

The shadows
That once populated
The busy sidewalks
Slipped away

*2*

The march of time
Made quick step
From then till now

And the turn of events
Made no mention
Of how

## Ray of Hope

Midst daylight
Or dark of night
An inner light,
Shines bright.

Follow
The Ray of Hope.

# Lamplighter

O Lamplighter.
You,
Lighting daylight
And midnight too.

Dark-ever-light
Light-ever-dark,
Lamplighter
And lamp
Never to part.

Lamplighter
Lighting

Ever.

## Go Slow

I've run through
  lots of nights
That didn't know
       slow.

Maneuvered
Around many days
      that
I only came to know
  in a hurried haze.

There's a time
  for going slow.

Tonight
Let's
Go slow.

## Nighttime

Stirring
The movement of creation

The full moon swoons lovers
And charms many others

Elsewhere

Sleepy eyes sleep
And dreams speak

## Flickering Flame

What of night
Does it light

This flickering
Candle flame


How near
Or how far

The star
Of which we are


What of night
Does it light

This flickering
Candle flame

## Intention

Brimming with intention
Surroundings mention
Life's wondrous bouquet

Live life
That way

# Metamorphosis

In the Stream of Life
The monarch
Settled for the night
On a maple leaf

In the Sea of Universe
Pages without numbers
Turn

## Poetry

Stars
In a universe
Of sky

And you
And me:

Living
Poetry

## Turns

*1*

Hummingbird
Coral Honeysuckle
Carolina Wren
Morning coffee

*2*

A road opens ahead
It closes behind,
I see the turns
Are mine

## Into the Night

When your noisy day
Gives way

To
Quietude

Be with me
Peacefully.

# Into the Night

## Clear Night

The sea of stars
We sailors
Sail

## With the Light
## Of the Night

Grant
The enchantment
Of moonlight
To you

Gift
Yourself
The universe
Of wish-giving stars

Gaze heavenly
And be
Completely

One
With the light
Of the night

## Counting

For those
    of you
     who
        question
Endlessness

Start
   counting
     stars

And when
You get to the end

There'll be
Stars anew

So,
Without end
     begin again

## Dream-light

The night
Gives sight
A magical light;
Every movement,
Every scene,
Every act,
In every dream.

## Stargazing

When we gaze
　　　at the stars
Is the light theirs
　　　　or ours

## There Goes
## Midnight

Tell me your name
I'll tell you mine
And
Where I'm from.

We can talk
About the weather
Or
The color of your eyes.

I swear
I've seen that color
In the Mediterranean Sea
And in evening skies too.

There goes midnight.

## Night Strom

The air ominous:
The roar of storm,
The strike of light,
The give of rain
Through the night.

## Wanting Eyes

Through the journey
Of the night

Some get lost
From lack of light

Some are found
In a light
Blissfully bright


Open the door
Just there before
Wanting eyes

## Faith

A lone train
Rolls through the night
Having
But a small light
To bright
The darkness.

Faith.

# Wholeness

*1*
Being
Is doing

*2*
The still pond
Reflects
The circle-moon

*3*
Depth

## Each Night
## Through

Each night
Through

Darkness
And we
Live

Symbiotically.

## Let Love Come

Let love come
Unfolding
Emotions
Warmly enfolding

# Goodnight

Relax

Ease
Into the darkness

No spell binding
Words
Nothing too complex

Life
Flowing
Free

Into the night

Goodnight

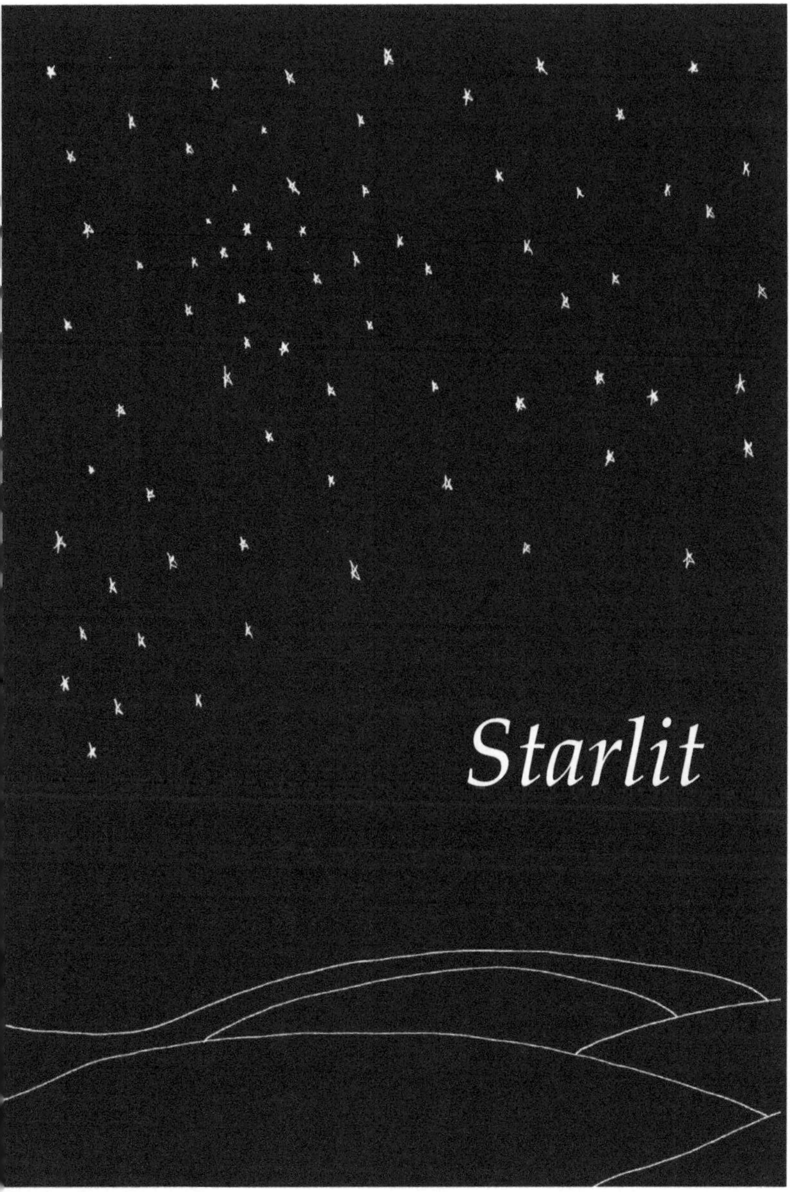

# Starlit

## All Starry
## Eyed

And so
If we say
      stardust

Are stars
    simply
    dust

And what about
           us

All starry eyed

# O
## The Love

In the darkness
Belonging to night

Where starlight dances
With the light of the moon
And the vast heavens
Sing in tune,

O
The love
Complete.

## Stellar

Heartbeats;

Call
Answer

Call
Answer

Call
Answer

. . .

## 2:22 AM
## Yellowstone

*1*

2:22 AM
February
Yellowstone, Wyoming

*2*

Darkness blankets the distant scenery
While at my feet, softly aglow,
Lies the powdery
New fallen snow.

*3*

The Milky Way hazes the night sky
Glorious the sounds, the sight -
Swirling, my thoughts
Swims the deep sky.

## 4

I, among constellations . . .

## 5

Voiceful steam
And murmuring stream
With Winter scene conversing.

## 6

Unnamed and untamed
The Winter winds
Blow in glory
Across Winter's
Starlit story.

## The Wading Pool

I've heard it said

"You're so deep"

But,
I am ever shallow

Wade me
You'll see


Forever yours,
*Eternity*

## Heavenly

Truth -
Travel to where
The stars are seen
Twinkling

And gaze

## Moondrops

A crescent
Amidst
A sky of stars:
Beauty.

A disk
Pale
Upon morning blue:
Calm.

## Tranquility

Tranquility:
Night
And me
In harmony.


In *Twilight: Awaking the Stars*

## As Lovers Say

Intimately
The days last sunrays
Make their familiar way
Through pastel clouds.

Shadows,
Promising night,
Lie softly
Upon
The naked city walls.

All
Goes by,
Paying no attention
To us
In this little room.

Stay with me
For a few more hours
Or as lovers say stay
Forever,

For I'll know you
Always.

## If You Listen Close

If you listen close
You'll hear

The breath of life
Near:

The sound
Of Love
Sincere.

## Midnight Eyes

Sometimes we sleep
Sometimes we keep
The night awake
All night long

Your midnight eyes
Tell your desire

Sleep's embrace,
Love's fire

## Passages

Nights,
That while away,

Days
That stretch along
Avenues
In between;

Passages.

## Dream

Dream with me;

    Lovingly.

## In Turn

The night
In its turn
Will let go
And leave
The earth it loves.

Just so
We will let go
Leaving
The arms we love
When night's gone
And morning
Comes on.

# NIGHT TO TWILIGHT TO BLUE

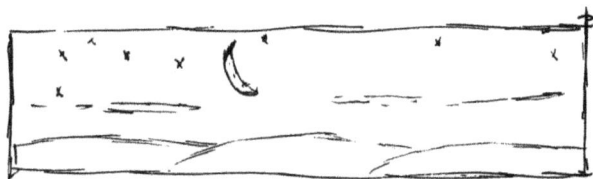

## Understanding

In the dark hours
I stumbled
And tumbled

But, I didn't fall
To pieces

Instead,

I came
To understand
I'd received
By giving
And grew
By living

## To . . .

The wind
The sea

The sand
Shifting

You
And me

Shifting
Too

Always
Shifting

To . . .

## Going Along

In graceful harmony
The falling leaves
Faithfully
Give themselves
With ease

To the season
Of cool breeze

## Of Memories

Here
A letting go

There
A wanting
To remember

Something dear
Recalled,

Something whimsical
Gone,

Something hidden
Beckoning

## Matrix

So much so

The navel of the world
Her dark toned nipple

## Daylight
## Moon

I remember us
Standing there
Surrounded
By soft
Early morning shadows
As darkness vanished
Swiftly
Into morning's light
And the daylight moon
Shined bright

## Eclipse

When
Did forever begin

Surely
It never ended

## Awareness

Awareness,
Boundless
Bliss

## Of Troubling Clouds

Be it night or day
When troubling clouds
Make their way
Hurriedly
Over our life sea

We

May call to mind

"Within there be
A harbor named
Tranquility"

There
Rest peacefully

## Wind Chimes

The wind blows
And the chimes
Chime -

Life is a miracle
And death is too

The give and take
Of me and you

True,
At times
We lose

But

Need be
We go on doing
What we forever do

**"Go On"**

## Kindness

Leaving defining lines
Behind

You find
Kind

# The Aegean

*1*

Winds
Gently
Embracing
Cresting waves

*2*

The color blue
 In lovely shades

*3*

How wondrous
The morning light
Dancing
Capriciously
On the Aegean Sea

## Dream
## By Dream

Love
Moves the night
Towards daylight,

Dream by dream.

## Life's Invite

At life's invite

We live the coming
We live the going

Distance
Indeterminate

## Worth the Doing

Harvest moons
Have come and gone
And will come and go
Again and again.

The singing of spring
Has teased
The summer sun
To fruition
And lulled
The winter solstice
To sleep
Many times over.

There's no need
To hurry,
All happens.

Go slow,
Wrap ease about you.

It's worth
The doing.

## Mi Amor

Mi amor
Your eyes

Filled with Love's light
Through the dark night

Easily
See

How much
I Love You

# Epilogue

## From the Mooring

*1*
Ebony
   quickly
     rushes through
       evening's rose-blue.

Dusk is gone;
      night is on.
Sleep draws near
       then sleep is here.

Having departed
   the dusky dock,
     sailors us all,
      in sleepy rhythm
           rock.

*2*

Borne on nights'
   dream-light,
      each sailor sails
        to a destined
          rendezvous.

There embraced
      by yesterday's
Insight
Then by love
Let go
   from the mooring
      of the night
        to sail into
        daylight.

# ABOUT THE AUTHOR

Inspired by nature and the beauty around him the multi-award winning poet Gary W. Burns started writing poetry at a young age. Early on Gary was able to express his thoughts, ideas and emotions through the vivid imagery of his verse. His poetry has been published in various literary arts journals, anthologies and magazines. He is the author of 10 books of poetry. Through his poems Gary shares his reflections on the many facets of life and on the beauty of nature. The expressiveness of his poetry has been enriched by his wide reading in philosophy and psychology. He has traveled throughout the world and has lived in numerous countries, to include, Italy, Korea, Saudi Arabia and Canada. He has also lived in Hawaii and several other states. Currently, Gary makes his home in Northern Virginia near the foothills of the Blue Ridge Mountains.

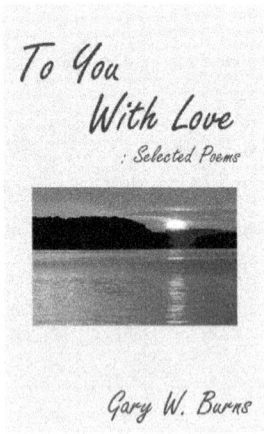

To You With Love: Selected Poems
ISBN: 978-0-9845342-6-5 (Paperback)
ISBN: 978-0-9827805-3-4 (Hardcover)
ISBN: 978-0-9860900-2-8 (E-Book)

Poems of Love: A Selection
ISBN: 978-0-9845342-8-9 (Paperback)
ISBN: 978-0-9827805-5-8 (Hardcover)
ISBN: 978-0-9860900-5-9 (E-Book)

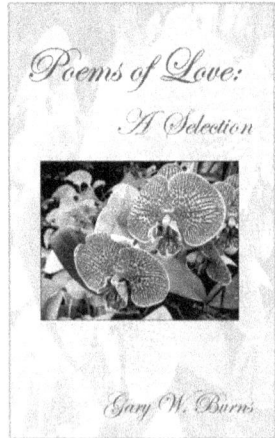

Dawn and Beyond: Embark
(Poetry - Come Destiny)
ISBN: 978-0-9827805-8-9 (Paperback)
ISBN: 978-0-9827805-9-6 (Hardcover)
ISBN: 978-0-9860900-0-4 (E-Book)

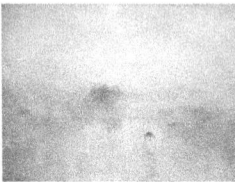

www.ingramcontent.com/pod-product-compliance
Lightning Source LLC
Chambersburg PA
CBHW021837020426
42334CB00014B/662